Chameleons

by Jim Lobes

illustrated by Larry Reinhart

Community Reading Partnership

Target Skill Short Oo/o/
High-Frequency Words they, you, of

PEARSON
Scott Foresman

Can you see the chameleons?

They sit a bit on top.

Can you sit a bit on top?

Can you see the chameleons?

They sit a bit in pits.

Can you sit a bit in pits?

Can you see the chameleons?

They sit a bit on top of rocks.

Can you sit a bit on top of rocks?

Can you see the chameleons?

Look, they nap.

8